MYSTERIES AND LEGENDS SERIES

MYSTERIES AND LEGENDS

OF MONTANA

TRUE STORIES
OF THE UNSOLVED AND UNEXPLAINED

ED LAWRENCE

TWODOT®

GUILFORD, CONNECTICUT
HELENA, MONTANA
AN IMPRINT OF THE GLOBE PEQUOT PRESS

A · T W O D O T® · B O O K

Copyright © 2007 Morris Book Publishing, LLC

TwoDot is a registered trademark of Morris Book Publishing, LLC.

Text design by Lisa Reneson, Two Sisters Design

Library of Congress Cataloging-in-Publication Data
Lawrence, Ed.
  Mysteries and legends of Montana / Ed Lawrence. — 1st ed.
      p. cm. — (Mysteries and legends series)
  Includes bibliographical references.
  ISBN 978-0-7627-4152-6
  1. Montana—History—Miscellanea. 2. Montana—Miscellanea. I. Title.
  F731.6.L39 2007
  978.6—dc22
                                                          2007003731

Manufactured in the United States of America
First Edition/Fourth Printing

TABLE OF CONTENTS

PREFACE

Before considering the mysteries and legends that lie between the covers of this book, you might want to suspend your preconceived notions about the nature of reality. Try to take these small bits and pieces of information (some of which require, admittedly, a leap of faith) at face value. Consider that, as far as we know, no one involved in any of these mysteries or legends is (or was) attempting to perpetrate a hoax.

For instance, when former Deputy Dan Campbell says that he saw dead cows in trees, we should try to believe him. After all, he grew up on a Montana ranch and was, at one point, a livestock inspector. Dan knows a cow when he sees one. And when members of the law enforcement community and the United States Air Force agree on the presence of unidentifiable craft occupying the space overhead, maybe their observations are worth a second look. In addition, consider a closer examination of the ghost towns Bannack and Virginia City even though these days the streets are pretty civilized, filled with browsing tourists.

It's easy to forget that in the 1860s these same streets were filled with prospectors looking for their fortunes and scoundrels (perhaps even the sheriff) interested in separating the prospectors from their money.

Lest there be any confusion, we're not trying to convince you that any of these mysteries and legends are real. But since it is mostly impossible to prove a negative (like the nonexistence of a monster living in Flathead Lake), how about we just agree that some of these mysteries are, well, pretty darn mysterious?

So sit down with this small sampling of tales from Big Sky Country and, if nothing else, let yourself be entertained. Forge ahead. Turn the page. Have fun.

CHAPTER ONE

WHAT HAPPENED TO MERIWETHER'S BOAT?

Should you decide to engage in a Montana treasure hunt along the Missouri River near Great Falls, Ken Karsmizki believes there's a chance you may unearth a 38-foot boat that once belonged to Meriwether Lewis.

Here's the background: Not long after the United States declared its independence from King George, Jefferson and his fellow newcomers to this land of opportunity began looking to the western horizon for new places to explore. Since most of the area west of the Appalachians belonged to foreigners, this meant some international wheeling and dealing. The end result? The Louisiana Purchase.

According to an agreement made with France and signed on April 30, 1803, for the bargain price of $15 million, the United States bought two million square miles of land, stretching from the Mississippi River to the Rocky Mountains. After the Senate ratified the deal on October 20, 1803, the Spanish, who had never relinquished physical possession of Louisiana to the French, did so in a ceremony at New Orleans. At a second ceremony the French turned the Louisiana Territory over to the United States, and Jefferson had the cat in the bag.

Thirty-year-old Meriwether Lewis, in addition to being a close personal friend to the president, enjoyed a reputation as a bright and inventive individual, an excellent organizer, and a tightfisted manager. When it came time for Jefferson to organize an expedition into the new territory, a "Corps of Discovery," Lewis seemed like a natural choice for leader.

To prepare for his expedition into the new territory, Lewis completed courses in medicine, botany, zoology, and celestial observation. He also studied the journals of those explorers who had preceded him as far west as North Dakota. In June he contacted William Clark, a thirty-three-year-old ex-army lieutenant and skilled river man, geographer, and cartographer with whom he had first become acquainted when he'd been Clark's underling. Clark was offered the position of co-commander, and the expedition was named the "Lewis and Clark Corps of Discovery."

The duo got along famously, perhaps because they were temperamental opposites. Lewis was introverted and moody; Clark was extroverted, even-tempered, and gregarious. The more refined Lewis, who possessed a philosophical, romantic, and speculative mind, was at home with abstract ideas; Clark, the pragmatist, was a man of action. Their relationship ranks high in the realm of notable associations, a rare example of two men sharing responsibilities in a dangerous enterprise without ever losing each other's respect or loyalty.

During the summer before their journey, Lewis oversaw the construction of an iron-framed keelboat he sometimes referred to as "a canoe." The virtue of it would be that it could be collapsed, carried along, and then reassembled as needed. Initial construction took place at Harper's Ferry, West Virginia, but turned out to be a bigger task than anticipated. Lewis wrote, "My greatest difficulty was the frame of the canoe, which could not be completed without my personal attention to such portion of it as would enable the workman to understand the design perfectly. . . ." From his notes we can discern the length of the boat to have been about 38 feet, consisting of six body sections, the stem, and stern.

The armature for the boat was eventually completed and shipped in sections to St. Louis. In the meantime Lewis took passage down the Ohio River, picking up Clark and recruiting expedition members along the way. By fall Camp Wood was established upstream from St. Louis and the corps had settled in for the winter.

On May 14, 1804, the company set off. Their group consisted of approximately forty-five soldiers and boatmen, and Lewis's dog, Seaman. By October they had arrived at the earthlodge villages of the Mandan and Hidatsa Indians, where they settled in for winter number two.

It wasn't until June of the next year that Lewis had occasion to try out his new boat. Scouting ahead of the main body, he caught sight of the anticipated Great Falls of the Missouri. The falls, however, were more extensive than he had expected. He realized that the expedition needed to portage around them. It would take a month.

There was another disappointment in store for him as well. He'd been planning to piece his boat together after the portage, covering the frame with animal skins. He wrote, ". . . Game becoming more abundant this morning and I thought it best now to loose no time . . . in providing the necessary quantity of Elk's skins to cover my leather boat which I now expect I shall be obliged to use shortly. . . ." And later, he added,

> on my arrival at the upper camp this morning, I found that Sergt. Gass and Shields had made but slow progress in collecting timber for the boat; they complained of great difficulty in getting streight or even tolerably streight sticks of 4½ feet long. We were obliged to make use of the willow and box elder, the cottonwood being to soft and brittle. . . . I have found some pine logs among the drift wood near this place, from which, I hope to obtain as much pitch as will answer to pay the seams of the boat. I directed Fraizer to remain in order to sew the hides together, and form the covering for the boat.

Nothing seemed to be going right for Lewis and his boat. He soon discovered that assembling the boat in the unpre-

Captain Meriwether Lewis and Federal Armory Superintendent Joseph Perkins inspect Lewis's assembled iron boat frame.

dictable conditions of the field was going to be much harder than he'd thought. Two weeks later, he wrote:

> This morning I had the boat removed to an open situation, scaffold her off the ground, turned her keel to the sun and kindled fires under her to dry her more expediciously. I set a couple of men to pounding of charcoal to form a composition with some beeswax which we have and buffaloe tallow now my only hope and resource for paying my boat; I sincerely hope it may answer yet I feel it will not. the boat in every other rispect completely answers my

most sanguine expectation; she is not yet dry and eight men carry her with the greatest ease; she is strong and will carry at least 8,000 lbs. With her suit of hands; her form is as complete as I could wish it. The stiches begin to gape very much since she has began to dry;

I am now convinced this would not have been the case had the skins been sewed with a sharp point only and the leather not cut by the edges of a sharp nedle."

Days later, he continued

. . . we corked the canoes and put them in the water and also launched the boat, she lay like a perfect cork on the water, five men would carry her with the greatest ease. I now directed seats to be fixed in her and oars to be fitted. The men loaded the canoes in readiness to depart . . . the wind continued violent untill late in the evening, by which time we discovered that a greater part of the composition had seperated from the skins and left the seams of the boat exposed to the water and she leaked in such manner that she would not answer . . . it was irreparable.

It is a sad day when a man loses his favorite boat. He later wrote:

base or just plain wishful thinking." Of the cargo-carrying capacity of the flotilla he writes, "The downstream flotilla had to accommodate only one half of the thirty-two members of the expedition because twelve members, including Clark, were more than 100 miles away on the Yellowstone River."

Enter into the debate Vic Reiman, a Lewis and Clark buff at the Montana Historical Society. In building his argument that the iron frame of the boat must have been traded to the Indians, Reiman points out that the 1806 portage of the Great Falls "was accomplished by 16 men, two teams of horses, and two low wagons or carts." (No horses were used on the portage the previous year.)

Reiman wrote, "Although Lewis told the portagers that he would meet them at the mouth of the Marias no later than the 5th of August, the men arrived at the Marias on July 28th . . . On July 28, when Lewis met his men on the Missouri above the Marias, he reported in his journal that all things had been brought safe: '. . . I now learned that they had brought all things safe having sustaned no loss nor met with any accident of importance. . . .'"

Reiman continued, "Neither Captain Lewis, nor Sergeant Gass, nor Sergeant Ordway reported in their journals that the boat frame had been abandoned (or reburied)." Later on the same day of their surprise reunion on the river, they all did report their inability to locate a cache with several beaver traps. Lewis and Ordway also recorded the loss through water damage of some beaver pelts and a robe in a cache near the mouth of the

Marias. The same day Lewis even recorded the loss due to water damage of some parched meal in a cache.

Reiman wrote, "Iron was extremely valuable as a trade item with the Indians. At Fort Mandan they had traded a 4" square from a burnt out sheet iron stove for 7 or 8 gallons of corn. . . . Although on July 28, 1806, they were apprehensive that the Blackfeet might have been pursuing them, they took the time at the mouth of the Marias to remove all the iron work (including nails) from the red pirogue, which was rotted out. They also recovered the blacksmith tools they had cached the previous year.

"I believe that Lewis buried his boat frame in 1805 with the intention of recovering it on the return trip and making it work right at some future time. Lewis wrote a detailed analysis of the reasons for the failure of his 'favorite boat' and suggested ways in which the iron frame boat might be successfully assembled in the future. If it were his intention to simply abandon the boat frame he could have accomplished that without the effort of taking it to pieces and securing it in its cache. With the current of the Missouri River to do the work, all that would have been required to deliver the boat frame to St. Louis would have been to carry it back over the portage and load it into a boat. The boat frame is estimated to have weighed about 200 lbs. and it would have been a simple matter to have loaded it into one of the canoes drawn on a cart by a team of horses. The boat was portaged up to White Bear in 1805 by simply placing it in one of the canoes on a cart drawn by men. To men who were used to carrying large quantities of meat over land back to their camps, 200 lbs. would not have been an unmanageably heavy weight."

To back his claim regarding Lewis's accounting methods, Reiman wrote, "Lewis used the common type of inventory keeping system in which items are logged in and out of the inventory. If an item is not mentioned one must assume that it has had no change in status. Once an item is logged in it is not necessary to keep repeating the status of that item. Some scholars argue that Lewis's dog, Seaman, did not complete the journey because he was no longer mentioned after a certain point in Lewis's journal. I think it is safe to suppose that Lewis would have recorded the loss of his beloved Seaman and, likewise, if the frame of his 'favorite boat' had been carelessly abandoned, Lewis would have recorded it."

In an interview in 2006, Karsmizki maintained simply, "They buried the boat because they didn't need it to go home." Karsmizki remains convinced that the boat is buried somewhere near Great Falls. "But the river is not stable and meanders, perhaps away from the burial site. Or, it could have been buried on an area that is now covered by a subdivision."

Either way, he says, "We still have not exhausted all of the possibilities."

Surprisingly, though the debate sounds acrimonious on paper, all of the participants agree that while the world of historical research is rife with disagreements, these debates are healthy. For his part Camp hopes that Karsmizki will eventually find the frame, despite believing that he's looking in the wrong place.

E. J. BASHOR

Rumors regarding a race of "little people" in the mountains of the West have been fortified by discoveries of mysterious mummies, like this twenty-inch-tall specimen discovered in a Wyoming cave.

these misfortunes could be blamed on the Little People and their invisible arrows.

A popular tale from the Pryors involves a child who fell from a travois only to be kidnapped and raised in a cave by the Little People. The lad stayed with his kidnappers until he became a man of superhuman strength. As told by the Crow Indians, he went on to build hundreds of piles of rocks in the Pryor Mountains. His biggest construction, called Medicine Rock, became home to the Little People.

To the Crow Indians, the Little People were protectors. Whether they existed as spirits or as flesh and blood seemed of little importance to this tribe. Stories are still told of how, during the days of intertribal warfare, the Little People would ambush the war parties of Crow enemies, tearing the hearts from the enemies' horses.

In a medicine dream Plenty Coups, the famous Crow chief, was led through the air from a high mountain by a spirit person who took him to a lodge filled with warriors of various, unfamiliar nations. He was shown that they were bad warriors intent on bringing evil into the world. With this knowledge Plenty Coups was able to avoid these miscreants.

Shirley Smith, owner of the Little Cowboy Bar and Museum in Fromberg, Montana, has been in pursuit of Little People history since she saw a mummy in school at age seven. Though personally having come close to a Little Person encounter on only one occasion, she has compiled a detailed library of Little People stories and anecdotes. She also numbers among her acquaintances at least one person who has had a visitation.

Among her historical documents is the story of two cowboys who, after being on the trail for three days, settled in around a campfire for the night. When one of them awoke to check the fire, he found that he and his sidekick were surrounded by a band of people that were no more than 3 feet tall. He didn't mention the visitation until, weeks later, a similar event was recounted by another cowboy.

Some tribal members also believe that the Little People can take on animal form, which fits with the story of Carson Yellowtail. During the winter of 1906, he and a friend were snowshoeing in the wilderness backcountry when his friend took ill. As Carson began snowshoeing out for help, he soon noticed that a wolflike or coyote-like animal was following close behind. The animal soon came so close that he occasionally brushed up against Carson. It was apparently herding him in a particular direction. At one point the animal kept Carson from falling over a precipice. When Carson finally reached a ranch house, the animal disappeared. Was it a Little Person in animal form?

Richard Myers, an acquaintance of Shirley Smith, recounted an incident that happened while he was attending a Mountain Man Rendezvous in the MacDonald Basin of the Absaroka Mountains. "During the event, Hash McDonald began playing flute music in an attempt to call the Little People," he said. At evening's end, the pair left a tobacco offering in their tepee, a common gift for Indian spirits. "Then strange stuff began happening. The emergency flashers on my truck began flashing, and I couldn't turn them off. For no reason, the valve of an oil tank several feet above the ground had been mysteriously opened and oil was being spilled. And we heard voices outside the tepee but weren't able to find any tracks." He also reported seeing a bright yellow light moving near the campsite, the origin of which was unexplainable. Myers was convinced that it was the Little People and that they are "rascals who like to mess around with vehicle lights."

On a separate occasion, during a spring bear hunt, he and his companions doused a campfire that they had built in a medicine ring. Upon their return a week later, they found the fire had been restarted, but there was no one in the vicinity.

Shirley Smith tells of traveling with four acquaintances to a picnic on the lower edge of the Pryor Mountains at noon on a sunny summer day. When they arrived at the deserted picnic site, they found a freshly constructed fire waiting for them (not what you might expect in the summertime). "But there were no other people around," she said.

She also spins the tale of an episode that involved an uncle who ranches in the Pryor Mountains. While he was digging an irrigation ditch with his tractor, a section of dirt collapsed, revealing a large cave. Returning to the site with a lantern, he discovered that three sides of the cave were filled with dirt shelves lined with the petrified mummies of Little People. Out of respect for the deceased, he covered up the cave and now refuses to divulge its location.

Most Indians in the area generally maintain that the Little People left southern Montana in the 1890s, their departure likely caused by the commotion of railroad and dam construction.

But they may have come back.

In 1991 two members of the Crow Tribe living near the reservation confided to Rich Pittsley, former manager of Plenty Coups State Park, that they may have experienced a sighting. They were surveying a shallow cave in a spiritual area near the

CHAPTER THREE

DID GOVERNOR MEAGHER GO SWIMMING?
OR WAS HE DROWNED?

The last time anyone saw General Thomas Francis Meagher, he was either floating, thrashing, or swimming in the Missouri River at Fort Benton late on the evening of July 1, 1867. How and why he ended up in the river has been a matter of conjecture for more than 140 years.

Upon his arrival at Fort Benton on that fateful day, the general was a guest for dinner (a midday meal in those days) at the home of I. G. Baker, a businessman with an office across the street from the steamer landing. Later in the day Meagher wrote a letter to his wife and then wandered the streets, eventually arriving at the dock where he boarded the steamer *G.A. Thomson* to spend the night.

According to Baker, at about 10:00 P.M., a company watchman discovered a man struggling in the river. Baker called for help. A group gathered along the bank looking for the late-night swimmer. In the meantime the watchman determined that General

A Civil War general and territorial governor, Thomas Meagher led a tumultuous, controversial life, aspects of which perhaps contributed to his death.

Territorial Governor Sidney Edgerton was fed up with the West. He'd had his bags packed for a return to Ohio even before Meagher's arrival. After the elected governor's resignation, the Irishman was immediately promoted from military secretary to acting governor. Republicans scornfully dubbed him "the Acting One."

Before hitting the trail, the previous governor was kind enough to share some facts of life with the newcomer: "There is no hope for your being appointed permanent governor because you are considered a Southern Democrat, despite your loyalty to the north during the Civil War. . . . You will have three enemies. The Sioux Indians, led by Red Cloud, the bravest, most vicious, cunning savage in the Indian nation who is bent on removing the white men from Montana. The Vigilantes. As a group they have gotten out of hand after cleaning up Alder Gulch and Rattlesnake Creek." And, "in your case, the Republicans." Sanders—both a Republican and an organizer of the Vigilantes—concluded: "There is no place right now on God's green earth that is rougher."

After this cheery introduction to his new home, the Acting One began his short stint as chief executive of the territory. Despite the backstabbing environment, he began to work in earnest, becoming something of a pen pal with the president. He petitioned Washington to appoint a surveyor general, requested the establishment of a postal system, and begged for an appropriation for executive and legislative offices, and the payment of overdue salaries to territorial officers. To defend against Indian uprisings, he proposed the establishment of a military garrison and a cavalry force of at least 850 men.

But Edgerton's prophesy about relations with the Republicans proved to be right. The hackles of his political enemies were raised when, in February 1866, Meagher claimed that it was within his power to convene a convention for the purpose of applying for statehood. Meagher may have had his eye on a United States Senate seat. But Sanders traveled to Washington, D.C., where he successfully convinced Congress that such an assemblage was unconstitutional. That was the first time in American history that Congress took unilateral action contrary to the legislative authority of a territory.

An unfriendly territorial judge also declared the convocation of Meagher's legislature a bogus act, his decision effectively writing *finis* to Meagher's first attempts toward Montana statehood.

Almost by accident Meagher also managed to incur the wrath of the Vigilantes. Having sprung up in the absence of legitimate law enforcement, this group of self-appointed executioners dealt unmercifully with suspected criminals. Their unauthorized, speedy trials were mostly conducted in the outdoors, close to trees, and with ropes.

In one incident a cowboy named Jim Daniels had enjoyed a lucky run at poker. When the drunken loser attempted to kill him, Daniels responded by killing the other man first. At the end of the skirmish, he hollered, "I'm innocent!" to a crowd of bystanders. Unknown to Daniels, that was a bad choice of words, since a local gang of highwaymen also allegedly used the same phrase to identify each other. The Vigilantes wrongly assumed Daniels to be a member of this disreputable group, and they took matters into their own hands by tossing him into jail.

Given the testimony of thirty witnesses who said that Daniels was innocent, Meagher commuted the cowboy's sentence and ordered him released. Not smart enough to leave well enough alone, Daniels returned to the saloon for a drink before leaving town. He was again apprehended by the Vigilantes. This time, however, he was strung up. A note pinned to the decedent's jeans announced that Meagher would be next.

Elsewhere in the territory Red Cloud was deciding he'd had enough of the white man's incursion into his hunting grounds and declared that it was time to eradicate the visitors from the territory. Given that threat, which resulted in the deaths of several settlers, including John Bozeman, Meagher petitioned the Feds for a small army and the guns to support them. After Washington agreed to ship a modest supply of arms to the territory, Meagher and an escort of six militia members traveled from Virginia City to Fort Benton to receive the arms. Coincidentally, while en route, Meagher met the newly appointed territorial governor, Green Clay Smith, another Republican from Ohio, at which point Meagher's title reverted back to general.

It's at this point that the history of Meagher's movements and behaviors becomes inconsistent. What we know for certain is that the former acting governor died in the Missouri River. The circumstances of his disappearance, however, are as cloudy as the river is muddy. The only witness to the event was an African-American barber on the steamboat who claimed that the general had let himself down from the upper to the lower deck and then jumped into the river without a word.

Months later, the crew of a steamer headed upstream reportedly found a body, but it was unidentifiable.

On July 7 the *Helena Tri-Weekly* stated, "He had retired to his stateroom, in which he remained for about ten minutes, when he opened the back door for some purpose, and it is supposed not using proper precaution, fell in. Our correspondent was on board the steamer *Guidon* at the time, which was lying below the *G.A. Thompson,* and heard the plunge, saw his head a moment, and then all was still. Every exertion was made for the recovery of his body but without success, and it is doubtful it will be found."

Here's a different version, from *Contributions to the Historical Society of Montana, Volume Eight:* "Meeting some friends on board, the evening was passed in a convivial manner, the [former acting] governor drinking deeply, and becoming intoxicated, when offended by some meaningless remark he grew angry and excited and charged some of the gentlemen present with desiring to take his life."

Then there was an article published in a 1928 edition of *The Eureka Journal.* "It is agreed by all who have investigated the events leading up to the incident that the general was temporarily

CHAPTER FOUR

WAS FRANK LITTLE MURDERED BY A COP?

Butte, Montana, in the early years of the 1900s, was one of the wildest cities in the West. A city of contradictions and conflicts, it was home to both some of the wealthiest capitalists in the world as well as some of the most irate socialists. Few people personified the conflicts of the day so well as Industrial Workers of the World (IWW) leader Frank Little and his nemesis, Sheriff Ed Morrissey. On either side of the labor unrest that roiled through Butte during its boom years, history tends to set the white hat on the head of Little, a wobbly (IWW member) and an Irish immigrant with a reputation for stirring up unrest among the working class. He became something of a martyr on August 1, 1917, when he was murdered by a team of unknown assailants.

The black hat lands on the noggin of Morrissey, who may have worn a badge but was decidedly an all-around bad guy, a disgrace to his honorable profession.

Frank Little, a senior member of the Industrial Workers of the World, came to Butte, Montana, looking for recruits. Instead, he found his own mysterious and tragic end.

tle's rants seemed to be advocating violence against ACM's property. This was considered a direct affront to the Anaconda Company.

The MMWU wasn't alone. William Dunne, president of the local chapter of the electricians' union, considered Little, "A very illiterate fellow, not very well informed on labor, who appeared to have a very bitter temperament."

Of note is the fact that in the days before Little's murder, many strike leaders had received threatening letters. Some were nightly changing their sleeping quarters. One IWW leader so feared an outbreak of violence that he left town.

The crime that Morrissey is allegedly responsible and most famous for occurred in the early hours of August 1, when a black convertible carrying a group of thugs parked in front of a boarding house on North Wyoming Street. Among the boarding house's residents was Little.

The masked occupants of the automobile made their way inside, where they announced their presence by breaking down the door to what turned out to be an empty room. Nora Byrne, the landlady, was awakened when the men began an assault on her door. It ceased only when she pointed them to Little's quarters.

In response to a question about their identity, they responded, "We are officers, and we want Frank Little!" It didn't explain their masks, but then nobody in the boarding house wanted any trouble. After kicking in Little's door, the thugs dragged him, clothed only in his undergarments, out to their waiting car. Mrs. Byrne later reported that she had seen none of the men's faces but believed them to be youngish, including one who was "short, chubby, and five feet four inches tall." These were approximately the same dimensions as Morrissey. It took Mrs. Byrne and two other boarders thirty minutes to decide that the episode deserved to be reported to the police.

Witnesses passing outside the boarding house during the fracas described Little being forced into the car, driven several blocks, then pulled from the car and tied to the back bumper, after which he was dragged for four blocks. He was eventually placed back in the car and driven to a railroad trestle behind an old smelter on the southwest side of town where he was unceremoniously hanged.

Shortly before sunrise, while en route to work, Robert Hall discovered the most recent addition to the railroad trestle. A placard attached to the victim's right leg bore the inscription in red crayon, OTHERS TAKE NOTICE. FIRST AND LAST WARNING. 3-7-77. L. D. C. S. S. W. T. The letter T was circled. In Montana's history, the numbers have a grim association, sometimes assumed to mean the dimensions of a grave that would measure 3 feet wide, 7 feet long, and 77 inches deep.

The following morning thousands of Little's friends, many of whom had cheered him at a rally just the day before, paid silent homage during a viewing of his bloody body at the city morgue. Later, 7,000 unionists joined a cortege that accompanied the body of the small man to his final resting place at "The

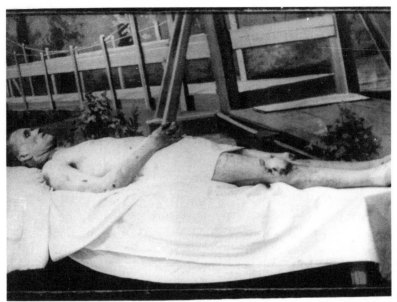

BUTTE ARCHIVE

Wobbly recruiter Frank Little was abducted from his boarding house by men claiming to be officers of the law. He was dragged through the streets of Butte before being lynched from a railroad trestle.

Flats," where he joined the company of miners who had died in the shafts, drifts, and stopes beneath Butte.

After the crime MMWU attorney William Sullivan named a laundry list of potential suspects, including "a member of the police force." All of his suspects were employed by the Anaconda Company. Sullivan maintained that the union would pursue justice, but his threat ultimately became idle chatter.

Theories regarding the identity of the perpetrators were in good supply. Little might have been murdered, for instance, by United States soldiers who didn't appreciate his antiwar outbursts. Additionally, folks speculated that he might have been killed by Metal Mine Workers members who were either in need of a martyr since they papered the city with photos of the deceased, or were opposed to his fiery rhetoric. The other rumors implicated the police and the Anaconda Company.

Of Morrissey's possible participation historian Jon Axline wrote, "Morrissey's long affiliations with the company and its hired gunmen make him a likely candidate for the murder of Frank Little." Following one of his dismissals from the force, Morrissey was hired in 1911 as a watchman for ACM, and between 1916 and 1919 drew a salary as chief of detectives while at the same time being on the payroll of ACM. This may explain the city's reluctance to pursue an investigation of Little's murder.

Undeterred by his bad press, Morrissey remained a scourge on the landscape. In 1919 he and a group of ACM guards terrorized voters and polling judges at two city voting spots. In the first, a drunken Morrissey assaulted an innocent visitor to the poll. Later, he assaulted three women ballot judges.

Morrissey's foul behavior continued for the balance of his lifetime. On the home front, he was accused of spousal abuse and the murder of his wife of four months, though the charge was not proven. He was convicted on several accounts of abusing the ladies at the poll and dismissed from the police force. In his last known public fracas he was reportedly involved in a dispute with constable A. C. Hocking, during which both had drawn their guns. Shortly before his death he was involved in a bar fight and was struck on the head by an unidentified assailant wielding a bottle.

The perpetrator left no clues, and the case remained unsolved until 2001 when an unrelated event presented a possible solution. This was when the Royal Canadian Mounted Police discovered a beaten and stabbed body in a frozen creek near Morinville, Alberta. With no suspects in the crime and without even being able to identify the body, the Mounties began circulating photos to law enforcement agencies and the media. Keen-eyed reporter Bill Morlin of Spokane's *Spokesman-Review* identified the deceased as a famous bank robber and escape artist named Kenneth Lloyd Pendleton, a native of Spokane.

Seemingly cut from the same fabric as John Dillinger and Pretty Boy Floyd, Pendleton was known in FBI circles as one of the most slippery and successful bank robbers in America's history. "He's truly a legend in Spokane," said one veteran investigator, speaking off the record. "He's the kind of criminal who commanded a lot of respect from police officers who knew him."

Pendleton was 6 feet tall and over 200 pounds. He once boasted that he could do sixty chin-ups without stopping. His criminal record began not long after his high-school graduation in 1959 when he was convicted of burglary. According to law enforcement officials, he robbed as many as eighty banks in at least eight states, challenging the FBI and law enforcement agencies to a lifelong game of catch-me-if-you-can. When incarcerated, he had a habit of escaping. In one case he somehow used mop strings and abrasive cleaners to saw through prison bars. In another instance he buried himself in a ditch on the grounds of

McNeil Island Prison where, for eleven chilly winter days, he lived off the milk of prison farm cows before swimming to shore. "He's one of a handful that have ever made it off McNeil Island, perhaps the only one during the dead of winter," Federal Probation Officer Bob Banta said at the time.

Back on the street, he was linked to bank robberies in Kettle Falls, Washington, and Pierce, Idaho, before being caught and sentenced to twenty-five years in prison. He escaped from a penitentiary in Bismark, North Dakota, and went on to rob $60,000 from a bank in Glendale, Oregon.

Following his arrest for that crime, he spent the next ten years incarcerated in Oregon. After being released, he is credited with robbing two banks in Spokane. After that his whereabouts were unknown until the discovery of his body.

Detectives from the Flathead County Sheriff's Department traveled to California to interview Pendleton's ex-wife, Arlene LaPierre. During a lengthy interview, Mrs. LaPierre told of being married to Pendleton at the time of the Easton murders and living in a cabin in close proximity to the Paradise Lodge. She had married Pendleton after their senior year in high school.

"And that's when the hell started," she said. "I was held hostage by him for three years or more, usually in backwoods cabins with no phone and no way to get out. In just over three years, we lived in more than twenty places."

Her husband was a thief, and he physically abused her. And then she added that she believed Pendleton was responsible for

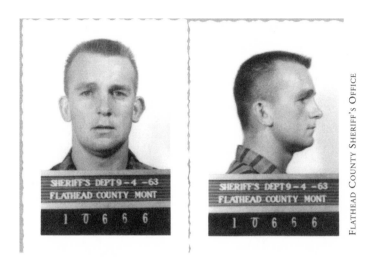

FLATHEAD COUNTY SHERIFF'S OFFICE

Later a victim himself, all clues point to Kenneth Pendleton being the murderer of Richard and Alice Easton.

the 1963 murders. "He returned to our cabin one day covered with blood," she said. "I asked him what happened and he said, 'I hit a deer. Don't ask any more questions.' He took his bloody clothes off, took them outside and burned them. That's the last time we talked about it."

LaPierre had later learned through news reports of the double murder at Paradise Lodge.

Records at the Flathead County jail confirm that Pendleton and LaPierre were in the vicinity at the time of the murders, Pendleton having been booked on a theft charge a few months later.

"We're fairly sure Pendleton is responsible for these homicides," said Maxine Lamb, who was then chief detective of the department. "Mrs. LaPierre told the detectives the same version of events, and added other specific details. Certainly, there will always be a question as to whether or not he really did it, because he's not alive to tell us that he did it. But with the information that has been provided by Arlene LaPierre, we're fairly confident."

But technically we're still left with two unsolved murders. We can assume that Pendleton was responsible for the murders of the Eastons. He had a motive, was in close proximity, and Mrs. LaPierre was a kind of witness. But the detectives have only circumstantial evidence.

And we're still left with the question of who killed Pendleton? And why?

Odds are we'll have to wait for the passage of more time to provide the answer to that question. Or we may never know.

CHAPTER SIX

WAS SHERIFF HENRY PLUMMER A HIGHWAY ROBBER?

Ask most Montana historians about Sheriff Henry Plummer and odds are pretty good that they will either describe him as a villain or a victim. He may have been both. In some eyes, Plummer was a prototypical, if mysterious, law enforcement officer. Others saw him as a wolf in sheep's clothing, living on both sides of the law, using his badge to help him in his crimes.

Regardless, Plummer found a permanent place in Montana's history books when he ran afoul of that infamous group known as the Vigilantes. On the lawless frontier of the 1860s, the Montana Vigilantes were a congregation of gun-toting, rope-slinging, like-minded citizens who decided that they were better administrators of justice than those legally appointed to the task. They were so confident that they managed to get away with hanging Plummer, the sheriff of Bannack, for the commission of crimes for which he had been neither legally charged nor convicted. Plummer was only one of dozens of people accused and executed by this self-righteous bunch. None of its members was ever arrested for what, in some views, were nothing less than murders.

Plummer's Jekyll-and-Hyde profile baffled historians more than a century later. In one view he was known to tip his hat to the ladies, act mannerly, and generally keep to himself.

In another view he was nothing less than a murderer. In a letter to the *Helena Herald,* Judge William Rheem said, "I remember Plummer very well. He was a quiet man and talked but little; when he did speak, it was always in a low tone and with a good choice of language. He never grew boisterous, and no impulse of anger or surprise ever raised his voice above that of a wary monotone. Affection, fear, hate, grief, remorse, or any passion or emotion, found no expression in his immovable face. With mobile and expressive features he would have been handsome—all except for the forehead; this, with the conformation of the skull, betrayed the murders, and Plummer knew it. I have said that Plummer knew he had a bad front; he therefore kept it jealously covered with the turned-down brim of his slouch hat. When he was not in the mood or act of slaughter or rapine, his politeness was notable and well timed."

Gentleman? Or scoundrel with a bad profile? Take your pick. Either way, his downfall began during the days when he lived a seemingly peaceful life as the sheriff of Bannack during a wild time in Montana's history. Bannack and later Virginia City, 70 miles up the road, were the sites of two of the largest gold finds in the West during the 1860s.

The birth of Bannack was strictly an accident. When a group of Colorado miners traveling to the overcrowded gold fields in Lewiston, Idaho, discovered quantities of loose gold along a creek bank, they began scouring the terrain for minerals. As luck would have it, they hit a jackpot. Word of the find spread quickly and miners poured into the area. Historians say that the area eventually produced quantities of gold that, as measured by the acre, rivaled fields in California and Alaska.

Like most mining outposts Bannack quickly became a rough place to live. Imagine muddy unpaved streets filled with crowds of money-hungry men who, in their spare time, had a seemingly insatiable appetite for whiskey, loose women, and cheap food, probably in that order. The smell of easy money also attracted opportunists, some of whom made their money honestly—by selling supplies to the miners, for instance—and others who took their gold at the card tables or at gunpoint.

Considering his history, temperament, and skill with a six-gun, Plummer was a perfect candidate for sheriff in a town looking for someone capable of bringing order to the chaos.

Prior to moving to Montana, Plummer had lived in Nevada City, California, where he'd had his first brush with the law. In that incident, he shot John Vedder, a lodger in Plummer's home. In Plummer's version of the story, Vedder had threatened him with a gun. Plummer shot him in self-defense. Mrs. Vedder initially supported Plummer's story. But then a local newspaper speculated that Plummer might have been motivated by a certain "intimacy between the widow and Plummer." This accusation was never proven, but Mrs. Vedder did later recant her support of Plummer's story. Plummer was convicted of murder and shipped off to San Quentin State Prison.

Eventually pardoned and released, he returned to Nevada City where, during a short stay, he was accused of pistol-whipping one of the locals, murdering William Riley while visiting a house of ill repute, and killing the owner of a dance hall in Oro Fino. Given the prospects of another in stint in prison, Plummer escaped from the local hoosegow and hightailed it north to Montana Territory. He was accompanied by Jack Cleveland, another miscreant.

The duo proceeded to Fort Benton, intending to catch a steamer to St. Louis. But while in Fort Benton, Plummer was smitten by the comely Electa Bryan (as was, not incidentally, Cleveland). Plummer delayed his departure long enough to marry Electa. The newlyweds then decided to settle in Bannack. Shortly after his arrival there, having made a favorable impression on the locals, on May 21, 1963, he was elected sheriff.

In handing the mantle of authority to Plummer, the locals may have, unknowingly, invited the fox into the chicken coop.

It didn't take long for Bannack's newest first citizen to make an impression on his constituents. Cleveland, unhappy at Plummer's besting of him in the courting of Electa, quickly became a weight around the sheriff's neck. He felt he had a modicum of leverage over Plummer by virtue of his knowledge of Plummer's

The grave site of infamous Montana lawman Henry Plummer

criminal background in California, which was unknown by the Montanans. Cleveland, fortified by this false sense of security (as well as a few jolts of John Barleycorn), had taken to publicly insulting the lawman.

During an argument with a fellow lowlife named Jeff Perkins and in the presence of Plummer, Cleveland accused Perkins of failing to repay a debt. When Plummer intervened on Perkins's behalf, Cleveland threatened Plummer. The sheriff drew his pistol, declared himself "tired of this," and shot Cleveland dead. Though he was eventually tried and acquitted of the crime (ruled self-defense), Plummer's reputation as a gunslinger was established. The incident also raised the eyebrows of the local newspaper. Local voters began reconsidering the sheriff's fitness for office.

Meanwhile, out on the trail, a new industry was emerging. As the wealth of gold was being transported out of the area via stagecoach, a band of robbers began taking notice. During a one-year period under Plummer's watch, more than a dozen stagecoaches were robbed, and one local was murdered by a highwayman.

Surprisingly, the behavior of the thieves made their identities common knowledge. By a strange coincidence they were typically broke one day and flush the next, their reappearance in town with pockets full of money seemingly corresponding with the timing of the robberies.

Their presence and behavior, coupled with the sheriff's lack of enthusiasm for putting the suspects behind bars, cast Plummer in a bad light. Was the sheriff involved in the robberies? He was a known acquaintance of many of the suspects. Locals also took note of the fact that his office was located in Chrisman's General Store, where miners sometimes discussed their travel plans. He was often out of town at about the same time that the stages left.

Eventually, in June of 1863, Deputy D. H. Dillingham began to suspect that his fellow deputies might be planning robberies. He confided his fear to other members of the community. Within days he was murdered by unknown assailants. But Plummer did not seem inclined to investigate the murder, raising further questions about his complicity.

Fueled by veiled accusations in the newspaper, public senti-
ment shifted. People began thinking that their sheriff was a crook,
even though his lifestyle had not changed and there was no hard
evidence that he had been present at any of the robbery sites.

Among Plummer's most vocal critics was Thomas Dimsdale, who wrote a number of articles incriminating Plummer in
the organization and management of the road agents. Dimsdale's
accounts were certainly biased and prone to exaggeration, especially since he had no hard evidence of the sheriff's guilt. They
also were tainted by a Victorian moralism that couched events in
terms of good versus evil. He described Plummer as "a very
demon who committed outrages against the laws of God and
man."

Dimsdale enjoyed scattered support in his criticism of the
lawman. A former friend of Plummer, Nathaniel Langford, once
said that he "lived in fear of his life," following a run-in with the
sheriff. In the summer of 1863, during a short-lived friendship
with Plummer, Langford was the president of the Union League,
the equivalent of a modern business club. Plummer applied for
membership, assuming that his friendship with Langford would
help him along.

Due to the suspicion that Plummer was engaged in the
stagecoach robberies, however, Langford personally rejected the
application. When Plummer learned of Langford's action, the
two engaged in a spirited discussion, at the end of which Plummer said, according to Langford, "You'll be sorry for this. I've

always been your friend but from this time on I'm your enemy; and when I say this, I mean it in more ways than one."

The threat may have been the trigger the Vigilantes had been waiting for. Dimsdale and Langford, along with a number of other prominent politicians and businessmen, were among the founders of the Vigilantes. They were embarked on a three-year crusade to round up, try, convict, and execute anyone suspected of criminal activity in the territory. They followed their kangaroo trials by immediately hanging their victims.

When an outlaw named "Red" Yeager was arrested, he was coerced into implicating Plummer as a road agent. The sheriff was corralled on January 10, 1864, at which time he is said to have begged, argued, and pleaded his innocence. But one of the Vigilantes responded, "You are to be hanged. You cannot feel harder about it than I do, but I cannot help it if I would."

Convinced that he was headed for the hangman's noose, Plummer's last words were, "Now, men, as a last favor, let me beg that you will give me a good drop."

Interestingly, following the hangings of Plummer and his alleged cohorts, the robberies did not cease. In fact, by some accounts, intelligence among the thieves seemed to pass more quickly, there was an increase in organized criminal activity, and more robbers were involved.

From an historical standpoint, there is no agreement as to Plummer's guilt. Was he involved in the nefarious activities of the highway robbers? Or was he simply negligent or inept?

CHAPTER SEVEN

IS THERE A CONNECTION BETWEEN UFOs
AND CATTLE MUTILATIONS?

You might not think that the deaths of a few cows would, in the grand scheme of things, mean much to Montana's history. But you'd be wrong.

Back in 1975 a sheriff's office in northern Montana received a phone call that two cows had been mutilated on a ranch near Belt. This was the first in a series of alarms that would affect law enforcement officials in five counties—and conspiracy theorists for years. In addition to signaling the commencement of one of the greatest unsolved mysteries in Montana's history, the call also changed the life of Captain Keith Wolverton of the Cascade County Sheriff's Department. He would eventually devote three years of his life to trying to find an explanation for the mutilations.

When Wolverton arrived to investigate the scene of the mutilations, the deputy discovered that the cows' bag, teats, rectal area, and reproductive organs had been removed, apparently cut out by an instrument with a serrated edge.

Perplexed, he sent samples of the mutilations to a pathologist in Colorado. The report read, "This strip of skin had a long, straight cut edge with regular serrations. Hair in one area had knowingly been clipped. Changes on the skin edge resembled neither tooth marks of a predator, nor those of wire lacerations."

Coyotes may feed on a carcass, but they don't leave a serrated edge. Magpies and crows might peck at the eyes, the rectum, any soft flesh, but they don't tear it away. Add that evidence to the fact that reports of possible cattle mutilations had first occurred in August 1974, and the deputy was confronted with a major-league puzzle.

Then followed a growing number of reports of similarly mutilated cows, the circumstances of which made things even more puzzling. All of the animals had been dissected in the same manner, but there were never any tracks near the carcasses, even in fields of soft, loose dirt. In one puzzling instance, the left jaw of a cow was removed, as was its tongue and right eye. In that case a veterinarian discovered what appeared to be a needle mark in the left leg of the victim. Had the animal been anesthetized prior to death?

When another event occurred in Teton County, Sheriff Pete Howard asked Wolverton, who was quickly becoming the resident expert, to assist in evaluating what might have happened. A Shetland pony was found lying on its side with all of its male organs removed. A veterinarian also discovered two puncture wounds in the horse's throat. And the body contained no blood. The ground was dry and unstained. "A horse this size should have had sixty pints of blood in its body," the vet said.

In a similar investigation, when another mutilated cow was found without any blood, an animal pathologist in Colorado opined that removing all of a cow's blood is virtually impossible since, when one third is removed, the veins collapse. Then he added, "It could be accomplished by injecting a saline solution into the heart while the animal is alive." This would also speed the rate at which the heart would pump. "Saline is virtually impossible to detect in an autopsy."

Over the next two years, an increasing number of reports were filed. One cow in Cascade County was found in a newly plowed field three-quarters of a mile from the nearest road or fence. But there were no footprints in the area. Miles away, another rancher reported the disappearance of a newly born calf whose mother had been mutilated. The calf was never located.

With a drawer full of similar reports, Wolverton had his work cut out for him. Organs were being removed with surgical precision. The lack of footprints or tire tracks eliminated cultists. There were no animal tracks or any signs of predation on the bodies. But maybe the animals had been injected with a needle. Wolverton enlisted the help of both a veterinarian and a rancher who wanted to see an end to the mutilations.

The rancher offered Wolverton a calf. The vet injected it with a drug that doubled the calf's pulse rate. Another needle in the neck drained the blood. As a result, they confirmed that all of an animal's blood could be removed. After a transfusion and when the effect of the drug wore off twenty-five minutes later, the calf was back on its feet.

When winter arrived in 1975, law-enforcement officers in five counties were being overwhelmed with reports of mutilations, all of which were following the same pattern. And Montana wasn't the only state afflicted with the same mystery. Reports of mutilations in Colorado, Utah, Idaho, and Minnesota were also making news. In May 1976 Wolverton began contacting law enforcement authorities in other states. Two incidents in Minnesota caught his attention. In the first a cow had been mutilated in an area covered by 6 inches of snow. A 6-foot radius of snow surrounding the cow was melted, though there were no footprints or vehicle tracks in the area.

In a second episode a pig was mutilated. The owner of the pig reported, "Last evening, my yard light went out, and I assumed it was burnt out. Then, about twenty minutes later, it went back on." He discovered the mutilated pig the following morning.

Back in Montana, dispatchers had received reports of unidentified helicopters. But on the day that the sightings had occurred, the wind was blowing hard enough to ground the choppers at Malmstrom Air Force Base. When Wolverton explained to Air Force officials that the residents were becoming antsy, they agreed to broadcast the message that their choppers did not fly after dark. There were reports of as many as nine helicopters flying together near Lewistown. By November 1975 even the Air Force was on alert. Helicopters had been sighted near missile silos, after all, and this was in the middle of the Cold War. Early one evening, a farm family observed yet another helicopter hovering over a silo, "So low to the ground that at times it seemed to touch," one observer said. It was spotted heading north near Dutton. Thirty-eight minutes later, it was at a missile site near the Air Force base. During a hectic four hours, sightings were reported over an area spanning more than one hundred square miles. An hour after midnight, an officer sent to investigate saw a strobe light flying east but could not verify that it was a chopper. A sergeant at the missile site added, "The object did not sound like a conventional helicopter, and had only a single strobe light and no running lights."

The object had appeared on radar only to disappear within 5 miles of the base. An hour later, Air Force officers reported seeing an unidentified flying object near the same area as the one that had appeared the previous night. Ten minutes later, a sheriff received a report of a UFO that did not appear on the Malmstrom radar. When contacted by telephone, the man who had sighted the aircraft reported, "Clouds are beginning to cover the object." He described the craft as having been very close to the ground. And it appeared to have a yellow appearance that turned white as it climbed.

More sightings, often of two objects, were reported the following evening, this time by officers on patrol. None of the aircraft appeared on radar screens. All were in close proximity to missile sites.

By May 1975 the Cascade County Sheriff's Office had received reports of 130 sightings in a five-county area. Many were confirmed as being helicopters, though the Air Force denied involvement. One was attributed to the Montana Air National Guard, another to a Canadian helicopter on a training mission. The officers also were told of sightings in fields from which cows were missing.

Some of the aircraft were described as being saucer shaped or like "a giant pear." Or like "a two-story building with lights resembling windows." A common denominator was the speed at which they traveled. A farmer from Raynesford estimated the speed at which a UFO ascended at 5,400 miles per hour. When the sheriff suggested that the object might be a star or planet, the caller responded, "Then why can I see a mountain behind it?"

Two teenagers reported to Undersheriff Jerry Skelton a strange object hovering over their car, "It continued to stay above the car as we hurried home." When they arrived home, they alerted other family members who went outside to view the UFO. "[It] hovered over their house before leaving a short time later," according to Skelton's report.

The list of sightings in 1975 is almost endless—and endlessly confusing. In some cases UFO sightings occurred in the same area as cattle mutilations. In one case a rancher saw a UFO land in an area where he'd deposited a dead calf. A day after the sighting, the calf was nowhere to be found. But perhaps the most compelling sighting was confirmed by NORAD. An oblong-shaped UFO was tracked on radar for more than an hour, during which time its elevation ranged between 8,000 and 18,000 feet. Then the object disappeared from the screen but was still viewed by deputies who had been dispatched to track it. When radar contact was reestablished, the object was at 14,100 feet, moving slowly. When the UFO was last seen it had ascended from 14,750 feet to 44,500 feet at approximately 1,000 miles per hour before stopping suddenly, then disappearing.

But once you scratch under the surface, it turns out that Montana has a long history of UFO sightings, beginning back in the 1950s. On August 15, 1950, in Great Falls, Nick Mariana was climbing the grandstand of the Legion Ball Park at 11:25 in the morning. As he neared the top, he happened to look north toward the smokestack. A bright flash caught his eye. Two silvery objects were moving swiftly to the south. "My first thought was, get the camera, they're flying discs! Then I thought again, they must be planes in a bank, and I'll see their wings in just a minute. Then as they got closer and more distinct, I realized there were no wings. These were not banking planes, they were flying saucers!"

Yelling for his secretary, who was in a nearby parking lot, Mariana ran down the stairs to get his movie camera. He was able to shoot about twenty seconds of 16-millimeter film before the objects arced to the southeast behind the General Mills water tower. In all Mariana and his secretary observed the objects for about three-and-a-half minutes. His reel of grainy color footage was among the first to capture flying saucers on motion picture film.

Described as a "reliable, trustworthy and honest individual [who] is highly respected in the community," Mariana immediately reported the sighting to the local newspapers. He also sent the film to Chicago for processing and showed it to several civic groups around Great Falls in September and October. In addition he loaned the film to officials of the Air Force's Technical Intelligence Center (ATIC). The Air Force concluded that the objects were likely reflections off a couple of F-94 jets that were in the area.

"The Air Force, however, returned only *seven* feet of the *eight*-foot film," wrote historian John Axline in his master's thesis at Montana State University. The missing footage showed the objects rotating in unison as they hovered over the refinery before continuing their flight to the southwest.

The "Montana Film," as it later came to be known, represented one of several UFO sightings in the Great Falls area in the early 1950s. On August 29, two men in the Geyser area reported seeing a "silvery mass" with a long tail. Two Great Falls Air Force veterans later spotted "six amber colored objects flying over the city." In June 1951 the *Great Falls Tribune* reported that "Heinie Wilson saw twelve round white objects while on U.S. Highway 87," about 50 miles northeast of Great Falls. The newspaper jokingly stated, "You know, for a while things seemed like the good

But Dan Campbell, who was raised on an area ranch, said, "People who dismiss the deaths are not looking hard enough. No vehicle tracks or footprints have been found around the animals. Cuts made to remove the tissue are very clean. There are smooth edges on those cuts. They are not bite marks."

Four years later, sitting over a cup of coffee in Choteau, Campbell still dismissed the predator explanation. Previously with the sheriff's department, he later became an investigator for the Department of Livestock. During that time, he saw "carcasses of cattle up in the trees on a ranch. They didn't climb up there. And we found dead cattle on the ground that had clearly been dropped from some type of aircraft because there was a deep impression on the ground." He also noted that the cow's skin "had a green glow to it." He attributes the fact that they were not eaten by coyotes or other critters to the presence "of some type of chemical."

Credible or not, there is at least one scientific explanation to the events of the 1970s and 2001. In the words of the "Summary Report on a Wave of UFO/Helicopters and Animal Mutilations in Cascade County, Montana, 1974–1977," published by the National Institute for Discovery Science (NIDS), Las Vegas, in 2002, the answer lies in a massive cover-up of infections that can be transmitted to humans by sick cows. The report states, "Although animal mutilation research has been immersed in a miasma of wild speculation, false claims, and unscientific methodology, there is considerable evidence that the phenomenon is real."

The two central and unanswered questions that have dogged research into this phenomenon are (a) Who? and (b) Why?

The conclusion of the report, taken at face value, is quite alarming. The authors propose that there is a link between the mutilations and the contamination of herds of cattle by a class of disease-causing agents known as prions—believed to be the cause of "mad cow" disease.

Further, the NIDS report hypothesizes that patterns of animal mutilations are consistent with a covert infectious disease–monitoring operation. Montana was not alone when it experienced the mutilations and sightings of strange aircraft. In addition to the scores of cases in northeastern Colorado, hundreds of other animal mutilation reports were investigated by local law enforcement in fifteen states, from South Dakota and Montana to New Mexico and Texas. Many anecdotal reports have claimed the presence of black or unmarked helicopters in the area of animal mutilations.

But why leave the carcasses?

NIDS says, "One of the most quoted hypotheses involves a government operation to monitor radiation or biological warfare testing. But the question, 'Why leave the body?' has never been adequately answered. The government can just as easily test their own herds, the counter-argument goes, or obtain carcasses from a slaughterhouse. For this and many other reasons, the evidence points away from the government as perpetrators of animal mutilations."

The report classifies the mutilations and abandonment of the bodies as "a brutal warning." It suggests that attention is being deliberately focused on the mutilated animals. "Further, we suggest the human food chain is compromised, probably with a prion-associated infectious agent that still remains mostly undetected."

In an even bolder statement, NIDS prophesies, "Mutilations will be followed, years or even decades later, by a TSE [mad cow] outbreak." And that "a rather large outbreak of CWD/TSE will occur in the area around Great Falls, Montana, in the next several years."

We have a tempest in a teapot. Given the Montana Film and the numerous UFO sightings, it is difficult to completely discount the presence, at one time or another, of UFOs in the skies above Montana. Perhaps space travelers were cruising the galaxy and decided to pay a visit to our planet? Regardless of their origin, the cattle mutilations are a fact that no one seems to be able to explain. The government hasn't stepped forward to confess, and twenty-five years of investigation has yet to produce a reliable conclusion.

We are stuck, it would seem, with what legitimately qualifies as a Montana mystery.

CHAPTER EIGHT

IF BIGFOOT EXISTS, HE NEEDS A SHOWER . . .

As if the Montana state police and sheriffs in five counties didn't have enough on their plate with the epidemic of cattle mutilations in 1975 and 1976, they were also being treated to an outbreak of Bigfoot sightings.

If you have not personally crossed paths with a Bigfoot, here's what you can expect to see, based on a random sampling of comments. He (or she) is a furry, gorilla type creature approximately 8 feet tall with dark eyes and the musculature of Arnold Schwarzenegger. The features are a combination of human and ape, with a wide nose, slanted forehead and flat, forward-sloping eyebrows. The head has a pronounced cone-shaped top. The neck is short, and the chin juts outward. The close-cropped ears are small and covered by hair. The skin on the face, hands, and feet is dark and leathery. The arms are long with the hands falling below the knees. In rare instances, both juveniles and adults have been seen walking on all fours.

The Bigfoot Field Researchers Organization (BFRO), a pioneer in Bigfoot study, lists 1,989 sightings dating back to the 1800s. Washington apparently holds the record for the most sightings in the United States, with 296 documented cases. Other contenders are California, 281; Ohio, 158; and Oregon and Texas, with 149 and 106, respectively.

Though the number of sightings in Montana pales by comparison with other states, there is an abundance of evidence that suggests the presence of these shy creatures in the Treasure State. If you run into him in the woods, however, and he doesn't respond to "Bigfoot," you might try calling him, "Bad Indian," "Mountain Devil," "Omaha Bushman," "Sasquatch," "Yeren," or "Yeti." Scientists have sometimes referred to him as *Gigantopithecus blacki,* an extinct primate that lived in Asia 300,000 years ago. Maybe he wandered to North America over a frozen Bering Strait, though Bigfoot literature is filled with theories regarding his origins. Because nighttime sightings are more frequent than daytime sightings, it's supposed that the creature is nocturnal. When a Bigfoot is encountered at close range, some witnesses report smelling a rank odor of rotting flesh, ammonia, or sulfur. The reports of the odor are so frequently connected to Florida sightings that locals refer to the critters as "Skunk Apes."

The first of Montana's sightings was reported on December 26, 1975, when a pair of high school students described to sheriff's deputies near Vaughn how their horses had been acting strangely that afternoon. When the girls ventured out to the corral to determine the cause of the uproar, they had seen a "strange creature two hundred yards from the house." One of the two kids grabbed a rifle—not to shoot the creature but to use the telescopic sight—and saw "a dark and awful face that did not look human."

When she fired the rifle into the air, the creature fell to the ground and began crawling toward a thicket of trees. The girls then observed several other, similarly grotesque creatures reaching from the thicket to assist their compatriot. After recounting their tale to deputies, both girls took polygraph tests. They seemed to be telling the truth.

Then one of their parents added to the mystery. He'd apparently been awakened the night before by a sound "like a human dying an agonizing death." People who see Bigfoot commonly report bloodcurdling screams associated with the sightings. About one month later, deputies were told by a man living miles away that he had heard a similar sound. And again, a few weeks later, a lady living in Babb had a comparable report.

Two months later, boys ages twelve and thirteen were near the Missouri River when one saw a hairy arm extending from the brush. The second boy saw a very tall creature covered with blackish brown hair and with eyes that glowed whitish yellow. When the incident was reported to Cascade County law enforcement officer, Keith Wolverton, both lads also passed the polygraph test.

Near Great Falls in March 1976, a fifteen-year-old boy reported seeing a hairy creature that he described as, "a

While most descriptions of Bigfoot tend to be strikingly similar, there is some variation, as portrayed here by artist Rick C. Spears.

ILLUSTRATIONS BY RICK C. SPEARS

Sasquatch-like thing" standing on Dempsey Road. Once again, the sheriff said, "The boy passed a polygraph test, no problem."

One of the most credible Bigfoot sightings in Montana occurred on April 4, 1976, when the critters began making themselves openly conspicuous. A sixteen-year-old boy living

Claus." And Dean of Arts and Sciences John Kijinski admits, "There have been grumblings about Meldrum's tenure, but no formal request for a review has been forthcoming."

Short of catching a glimpse of Bigfoot ourselves, however, the rest of us are left to wonder, is he real or imagined, is he Yeti or *Gigantopithecus blacki?* Or maybe pranksters have been dressing up in Halloween costumes. But it is hard to dismiss the number of independent, unrelated sightings reported over the years, most of them by individuals who don't seem to care for fame or fortune.

One sure fact remains, however: If Bigfoot does exist in Montana, he needs a shower.

CHAPTER NINE

WHO NAMED THE CRAZY MOUNTAINS?

If measured by the height and number of spectacular peaks, not to mention downright beauty, the Crazy Mountains near Big Timber may be the most underrated mountain range in the Rockies. Often referred to as the Crazies, they have a tendency to collect mysteries.

Located between the Musselshell and Yellowstone Rivers, the range rises more than 6,000 feet above the plains to the east. Running for 50 miles north to south and 15 miles east to west, they dominate their surroundings, plainly visible for miles from Interstate 90, Highway 89, and Highway 287.

The mountains' first human inhabitants were Stone Age hunters. An archaeological dig on the west side of the mountains unearthed a site that produced tools thought to have been used more than 11,500 years ago. The next known occupants of the area were the Shoshone Indians, who set up camp about 1,000 years ago. The Shoshone weren't very warlike so when the Crow and Blackfeet tribes, and later, white men, arrived on the scene, the Shoshone packed up and departed.

Since Lewis and Clark left their footprints in nearly every other zip code in Montana, it only makes sense that they would have passed through this area, though these mountains remain one of the few landmarks they did not name. While following the Yellowstone River where it runs near the foothills of the mountains, William Clark camped at the confluence of the Yellowstone and Shields Rivers on July 15, 1806. The following night he and his party slept at "Rivers Across" near Big Timber, the spot where Otter Creek and the Boulder River flow into the Yellowstone.

So, who is responsible for naming these spectacular peaks?

Archaeologist Larry Lahren tells us, "The Crow Indians called them the Mad Mountains because of their steepness, rugged beauty, and haunting winds." Other Crow names for peaks in the Crazies are Awahawapiia (Rugged Mountains), Bird Home Mountains, Mean Mountains, and Blue Bird Mountains. They referred to the tallest peak as Ahwahhawa Peak, which means Mad Mountain. The Crows believed the mountains to be inhabited by angry and vicious spirits.

It might also not be a coincidence that the flora and fauna of the area includes loco weed, a toxic plant that can sicken livestock if they eat it, turning them confused and disoriented.

Even the geology of the mountains adds to the mystery of the name. Rocks in the southern part of the mountains tend to be composed of sodic plagioclase, biotite, hornblende, and augite,

One of southern Montana's most striking landmarks, the Crazy Mountains are visible for miles from every direction.

while in the northern part of the range they are augite, olivine, biotite, alkali feldspar, and sodalite. Geologists are still trying to solve the mystery of how two entirely different rock types came to form the same mountain range.

Yet another theory is that the mountains were named after a member of the Crow Tribe. In this version, a woman who went mad moved to the mountains and sought refuge amidst the peaks. They became the "Crazy Woman Mountains." Legend has it that members of the tribe became her caregivers. Similarly, in his novel *Mountain Man,* Vardis Fisher penned a character named Sam Minard, an intellectually minded loner. His character was patterned after the real-life mountain man John "Liver Eating" Johnson. In Fisher's tale, during one of his hunting excursions around the Yellowstone River, Minard came upon a tragic scene. While in her cabin cooking dinner, a woman named Kate Bowden had heard the screams of her children. Rushing outside, she discovered that her husband and two sons had been brutally murdered by Indians and the attackers were raping her daughter.

Fisher describes Bowden turning upon the attackers. "She moved with such devastating speed and her blows were so unerring that four warriors fell before any of them realized that an avenger was upon them." When the carnage was over, "Kate Bowden stood, shuddering with rage and tremors and lunacy, her dead children and four dead Indians around her."

Sam Minard comes upon Bowden and, ever the good Samaritan, finds a shovel in her camp and is about to begin digging graves, when "she came running toward him, gesturing, like a mute. He followed her and she climbed to a tableland that was high enough to overlook the river and its bottom. . . . She took the shovel and marked off three spots. Then, convulsed, it seemed to Sam, by frustration or anguish, she fell to her knees."

In the years to come, and on the many occasions when he was near the Yellowstone, Minard checked on Kate's condition. They never spoke, and she rarely acknowledged his presence as her mind drifted farther from reality. He usually killed a deer or two for her larder and provisioned her cupboard at the beginning of every winter.

On his last visit he toted a sack of wildflowers for her spring garden. "[He] came to the hill where he had always paused to look at the shack and the garden and cried aloud 'My God!' and some part of him died. He saw the second cairn of stones, standing close by the one he had built, and he knew that Kate was dead."

Did Vardis Fisher somehow unveil the true history behind the name of the mountain range? Or did the name arise from the account of the Crow Indians?

Whatever the source, Spike Van Cleve probably got it right when he wrote in *Forty Years' Gatherin's*, "It's a good country. Where a man can sit in his saddle and see all across to the west stretch the Crazies, and swinging in the stirrups, a man has to throw back his head to follow their abrupt shoulders up to the white crests of the peaks."

That pretty much sums it up.

on Flathead Lake for more than thirty years, does not dismiss the possibility. "It is scientifically possible that there is something in the lake," he said.

Those fortunate enough to have seen Flessie in action have described the monster as being between 8 and 20 feet long, with gray to black coloring, and having three or more humps on its back. When moving on the surface, the monster creates a wake 8 to 12 inches tall, about the same as a powerboat.

While taking samplings of life in the lake, Hanzel experienced "several occurrences of my net being damaged. It had big holes in it that we can't explain."

Of the reported sightings, he said, "I think they are as real as people say they are. I've interviewed people and, without asking any questions, just listened to their descriptions, and they are all remarkably similar in describing the behavior and appearance of the creature. Many of them occurred during the evening hours, and were preceded by the sighting of a school of fish flying across the surface."

Hanzel has tallied eighty-one different accounts, most of them describing an eel-like monster "with humps and smooth skin. . . . I don't know what the thing is. It could be something from prehistoric ages."

In 2005 Paul Fugleberg of Polson, former publisher of the *Lake County Leader* and author of a booklet entitled *Montana Nessie of Flathead Lake,* has chronicled every sighting of the monster since 1889. Many of the sightings occurred near the Narrows on the south end of the lake, near Polson, and around Wild Horse Island. In August 1947, as Fugleberg describes it, a dozen people observed a huge fish estimated to be 20 feet long, brown, shaped like a fish. Later that same month, other witnesses "observed a large fish estimated to be about 20 feet long, and very fast, that remained in the area for a while before disappearing." Multiple sightings have been reported annually, the only exception being 2004.

Most accounts are very believable and include sightings by two or more witnesses. For example, in March 1953, fifteen mill workers watched "a big fish swimming about 200 yards from the Polson waterfront." Two years later, when Mr. and Mrs. Neil DeGolier thought they saw an overturned boat on Skidoo Bay, "They could see it was a huge fish that they watched roll on the lake surface for several minutes."

The spring and summer of 1963 were good years for Flessie sightings, as several families, and two high-school teachers, in separate sightings, saw "a dark gray object with three humps" and "a seven-foot-long fish cavort playfully in the Narrows."

Two of the most detailed accounts come from a Major George Cote in 1985 and 1987. His first sighting was in Yellow Bay. "We saw a large object surfacing and diving off the north point. We approached the thing slowly. As we got close, we could see it was chasing squawfish in the shallows. At one point it raised its head high and appeared to be looking at us.

"When we got to within 60 meters of it, we realized that it

was nothing we'd ever seen. The thing was big: as long as a telephone pole and twice as large in diameter. The skin was smooth and coal black; it had the perfect head of a serpent. There were four to six humps sticking out of the water. It moved away from us slowly, then took off like a streak."

The second sighting occurred on July 1, 1987. Major Cote said, "I've caught bluefin tuna over 1,000 pounds. I've seen sturgeon. I've been out on Flathead Lake over 300 times in the last 25 years, and I know what a submerged log looks like. I know what I saw. There's no doubt in my mind that it was a huge creature."

Most recently, an August 2005 report in the *Bigfork Eagle* recounted the experience of Polson attorney Jim Manley and wife, Julia. The couple was taking a snooze aboard a boat anchored in Big Arm bay early one evening. "We began hearing rhythmic splashing," Julia says. "Then we saw a mysterious oddity splashing for several minutes in Big Arm Bay. It was loud. After about three splashes we both opened our eyes and looked out on the water and then at each other to see whether we were seeing the same thing."

"It had a serpentine look," Jim added, "with several humps visible above the water. It moved slowly away from shore toward Wild Horse Island." Both agreed that "it wasn't a log, and it was moving against the current. The wind was a little breezy, and the lake was mostly calm except for the splashing of the dark-colored thing."

"It was something very large," Julia said.

They watched it for two to three minutes and judged it to be about 25 feet long. It was 75 to 100 yards away. A few feet separated the rounded humps as they rose nearly 2 feet out of the water. "It wasn't an optical illusion," Jim said. "The part above surface looked about as long as our boat. What really struck us was how loud the splashing was. It was regular, like waves breaking on a beach."

On the same day that the Manleys reported the incident, Hanzel was taking the report of a second sighting. Three-year-old Andrew Johnson had a real life encounter with Flessie, or says he did.

While Andrew's mom, Cindy, and Cindy's sister were preparing for a boat trip on the lake, Andrew headed for the water on his own. Walking down to the dock, he took an unplanned dip into the lake. His mother flew into a panic. The youngster didn't know how to swim, and he was literally in over his head.

But within seconds, Andrew had been hoisted back onto the dock by an unknown and unseen rescuer. In his words, "the Flathead monster lifted me up with his tail."

A lad of few words, he added, "She has a baby, too."

So as far as Andrew is concerned, not only is Flessie real but it has started a family, too.

enveloped in the mystery of the prison. "Visitors to the prison often produce unsolicited comments about unusual experiences. One lady on a tour came out of the solitary confinement cell, took me aside, and asked if someone had died in that cell. She said that it had the feeling of death." (For the record, no known death occurred in that space.) "And a photographer who was on his own left earlier than he had planned after telling me that the solitary confinement cell was 'filled with evil.'"

The prison's history isn't one of the brightest spots in Montana lore. When the territory's bad apples became too great a nuisance, the legislature requested funds from the federal government in 1866 for the purpose of constructing a prison. While Congress agreed that the territory needed a prison, the funds they allocated for the construction were inadequate.

It wasn't until July 2, 1871, that the prison was finally finished. On that day Samuel Hughes became Deer Lodge inmate number one. His sentence for assault with intent to kill was nineteen years, but because the prison had only fourteen cells, he was pardoned by the governor and released six months later. Like a game of dominoes, every time a new inmate arrived a current resident was pardoned, even though the convict being released might have been more dangerous than his replacement.

As the state's population increased, it enjoyed a corresponding increase in the crime rate. Overcrowding at the prison became a chronic problem. It would be a century before the original facility was abandoned in favor of a replacement facility 5 miles west of town.

Before its closing, though, two more hoodlums and a new warden would add their stamp to the facility's unfortunate history. When Jerry Myles and Lee Smart, two career criminals, and Warden Floyd Powell arrived in 1958, discipline was in a shambles. Powell wrote that the use of pills and narcotics was rampant. He described gambling, payoffs, and "other nefarious activity."

Before taking residence in Deer Lodge's old prison, Jerry Myles's forte had been burglary. He had been in and out of various prisons since the age of ten. Acclimating to Deer Lodge, he quickly became a "con boss," a king of the hill, and a homosexual predator. With the arrival of Powell and the new deputy warden, Theodore Rothe, in 1958, Myles was often consigned to solitary confinement, where he spent many lonely hours plotting revenge.

Myles's coconspirator, Lee Smart, was already a convicted killer and was willing to kill again in order to escape confinement. By the afternoon of April 15, 1959, a Thursday, the duo had recruited several convicts to stage an uprising, which they hoped would result in their freedom.

In short order, they overcame the guards in their cellblock by dousing them with flammable naptha stolen from the garment shop. They then commandeered the kitchen, as well as the second cellblock, and strolled casually to the administration building. There they overpowered guards and took the entire staff hostage. Unaware of the revolt, Deputy Warden Rothe was sitting behind his desk when Myles and Smart arrived, taking him by surprise. Smart killed Rothe with a rifle shot through the heart.

Warden Powell, who was outside the prison walls at the time of the uprising, began negotiating the release of twenty-one hostages. After a thirty-six-hour standoff, on Friday evening the warden decided that the time had come to retake his facility. With assistance from the National Guard, he led a successful assault on the main gate. After the hostages were freed, his focus shifted to Myles, Smart, and three other convicts who had taken refuge in the northwest guard tower. At Powell's urging the three tagalongs surrendered, leaving Myles and Smart on their own.

The two ringleaders made their decision quickly. When the guard stormed the tower, Smart shot Myles, then committed suicide.

It was into this history that we interjected ourselves for the anniversary tour. Shortly after our arrival, Kris began recounting events from the previous evening's walk-through. One young lady who had been alone in the prison's darkened theater felt her hair being pulled from behind. In another part of the prison, she had also described an "eerie feeling." And during the wee hours after the visitors left, TSI's infrared recorders filmed the presence of unexplainable patterns of light in the same area.

With appetites whetted and blood pressures slightly elevated, we began our tour at the prison's administration building, scene of the Rothe murder, a site at which orbs have been observed. The routine was simple. Enter an area where activity could be anticipated, sit, then wait and observe. While we were in the administration area, a sudden twelve-degree drop in temperature was recorded by an infrared thermometer. The temperature returned to normal again within seconds.

"That is generally agreed to be a sign of an unknown presence," Eric said.

The next stop, the main cellblock, included solitary-confinement cells, and the maximum-security cellblock, sites at which paranormal events have been recorded.

Kris said that the darkest region of the main cellblock had frightened him more than any other area of the prison. While we waited silently for some evidence of an unseen visitor, another tour member took a series of random photographs near cell number forty-six, a flash attachment illuminating the dark. When we viewed the photos on the camera's digital display, they clearly showed an orb about the size of a soccer ball directly over Julia's head. From that point on, everyone on the tour seemed to be walking on eggshells.

"Definitely something going on there," Kris concluded. He did not have to ask a second time if we were ready to move on.

After touring the maximum-security cellblock, we came to a cubicle attached to the exterior of the building, a site place where inmates had been allowed to receive visitors. The previous evening the exterior door had, without the aid of wind or human intervention, opened itself. And following the departure of tour members, lights that had been turned off were mysteriously turned on.

We experienced our own scary moment. As we stood outside the cellblock listening to Eric recall the previous night's events, we clearly heard the clanging of a closing metal cell door from deep inside the prison.

When three of us returned to the cellblock, we confirmed that there were no living humans inside. Eric had previously explained that this was the same cellblock in which voices had been recorded by ghosthunters from Seattle.

Undeterred by the unexplainable sounds, I returned to the cellblock with Patrick Straub, another member of the tour group, and Eric, who shot footage with his video camera. "We may be recording something, but will not see it until we play the video," he said.

Patrick did see something. Or thinks he did. "I just saw an orb at the lower corner of that cell," he said anxiously. "Or something like that."

After the stroke of midnight, on the anniversary of the riot's end, it was with great anticipation, and some apprehension, that we headed up the narrow, winding stairway to the fourth floor gun station from which Myles and Smart had departed this planet. After listening to Kris's patient attempts to arouse the spirits—"Is anyone here? Is there anything you want to say to us? Can you give us a sign?"—we concluded that, if there were any spirits in the area, they had taken the night off.

The Bratliens aren't the only ones investigating paranormal activity in Montana. Ellen Baumler comes to the subject as an historian. When asked to investigate the presence of a spirit in a home or other site, she apparently takes a skeptical, but open-minded, approach. Her approach is first to unearth the history of a property and its former occupants. If she can determine a possibility for paranormal presence based on historical fact, she forges ahead.

In her book, *Spirit Tailings,* her story, "The Body in the Bathtub," serves as an excellent example. It seems as though a respected matron named Lucille lived alone in a large house in Virginia City from the 1940s until the 1980s. During the latter years of her occupancy, she had taken to rambling about a "horrific, bloody apparition that occasionally manifested itself" in her bathtub. She eventually became so irrational that the locals began referring to her as "Loose Wheel." Exhausted by the stress, she eventually sold the property and moved on.

The new owner did some sleuthing, however, and eventually compiled a history of the house. Prior to Lucille's arrival, it seems that the house was owned by a married couple from Chicago. The husband was robbed and murdered by road agents. In 1905, after a second couple took ownership of the property, this husband also died and, following his death, the despondent widow committed suicide in the bathroom.

More than twenty similar stories are contained in the pages of Baumler's books, causing skeptics to pause before totally discounting the possibility of spirits. (An aside: Though she is reluctant to discuss the matter, the house in which the Baumler family resides has also been certified as having ethereal spirits within its confines.)

Other examples include the Crowne Plaza Hotel in Billings, formerly the Sheraton, where an elevator has been known to call the front desk for service at 2:30 A.M. However, neither the front desk manager or security guard has been able to learn who's making the call.

Chico Hot Springs Lodge and Resort is a Montana landmark. It combines the charm of an historic hotel with the environment of a hot springs and dude ranch. Some of its former guests were so taken with the place that they have, apparently, extended their visits past the grave. In May 1986, two night watchmen came upon the airy form of a young woman hovering near a piano in the third floor lounge. The face of the apparition lingered long enough to allow a guard to snap a photograph. As typically happens, when the film was processed, only a tiny white spot appeared. While this was not the first time the "Lady in White" had been seen, it was the first time that she had allowed herself to be photographed.

Four years later, two other guards followed the Lady from the lobby to the hallway leading to room 349, where her presence has been reported by many employees and guests. There's also a rocking chair in room 349 that, regardless of its initial location, eventually ends up facing a window.

In Virginia City, the Bonanza Inn was the first county courthouse in Virginia City but was replaced in 1876 and converted to a Catholic Hospital. Next door, Bonanza House was later con-verted to a nunnery. The ghost of a nun has appeared in both places. Furthermore, one room at the inn is now sealed because of a series of frightening poltergeist manifestations. The appari-tion of a lecherous man has appeared in one of the upstairs rooms at the Bonanza House. Mysterious footsteps, strange feel-ings of discomfort, and bone-chilling cold spots are common occurrences.

At Bannack State Park in Dillon, the park's assistant man-ager, Tom Lowe, has a ghost story of his own. It seems as though the residents of Bannack have an annual Halloween Walk. It's an opportunity for participants to paint their faces in a ghostly motif, dress up like the ladies and gentlemen who resided in the city in the 1860s, and generally have a grand time. In 2001, how-ever, they discovered that they might not be alone. At the end of the evening's festivities, many of the participants gathered for a group photo. When Lowe had the film processed, he discov-ered that an uninvited image had barged into his viewfinder. "That's not a person, or a reflection from a bright object, or any-thing we can explain," he said. "It does look something like a ghost, doesn't it?"

Shirley Smith of Fromberg, in addition to being preoccu-pied with the Little People in the Pryors, is also the proprietress of the Little Cowboy Bar and Museum. During our first meet-ing, she casually mentioned the frequent appearance of Hank Deines, the former owner of the bar. Hank's presence in the bar continued for years after his death, and Ms. Smith wasn't the only recipient of his attention.

Hank, it seems, died in 1971 while lying on a cot in a back corner of the bar. Ms. Smith subsequently purchased the establishment from Hank's widow, Mary, who later moved to Billings. Hank's spirit, however, seems to have remained in Fromberg.

Ms. Smith recalled a disconcerting evening, "There were three customers sitting at the bar. I was filling glass mugs that hang on cup hooks on the wall with peanuts. They are on hooks, so very secure. All of a sudden, the cups flew up into the air, dislodged one of the ceiling tiles, and landed on the bar without breaking a mug!"

She continued, "An employee named Teaia was working the late shift and, while handling cleaning chores, was playing music very loudly. That apparently disturbed Hank because Teaia began hearing a dull pounding sound on one of the tables. When she ignored the sound, the pounding increased in tempo and velocity, at which point Teaia said, 'OK, Hank, I'll turn off the music.' She did, and the pounding stopped."

Hank's visits apparently stopped in 2003. "But he returned in 2006," Shirley said. "Or someone did." Light fixtures seemed to have taken on a life of their own. "They are turning themselves on and off. The same is true of some of the machines. . . . And our security guards have seen people in the building in the middle of the night, long after we've closed and the place is empty. Is it Hank? It could be him, or someone else who likes the place. Whoever it is, I kind of like having him around because, so far, he's been harmless."

Considering the number of level-headed, educated Montanans who have had experiences with the paranormal, it's hard to ignore the possibility that we might share our space with the dead. So the next time a teacup falls from the mantle for no apparent reason or the dogs start howling, you might want to reach for the video recorder. Or at least find a safe spot under the sofa.

EPILOGUE

A SHAGGY DOG STORY PRODUCES A MYSTERY

So there you have it, a smattering of mysteries and legends from the Treasure State. Given the number of sightings of Unidentified Flying Objects, we have to wonder: Is Montana's famous Big Sky filled with more than commercial, recreational, or military aircraft? And what about Harry Plummer? Was he an honest sheriff wrongfully murdered or was he himself the leader of a gang of bandits? And if he was crooked, where did he hide his loot? Then there's the mysterious death of the former governor, General Meagher, in Fort Benton. Did a sick man fall overboard while answering the call of nature or did he kill himself? Or was he the victim of Vigilantes? And what about paranormal spirits? It becomes increasingly difficult to argue against their existence, especially since so many people who have no connection with each other have experiences with uninvited guests. If you're a skeptic, spend an evening with the Bratliens during a midnight tour of the Old Prison, and you might be surprised at how your thinking can change. Then there are all those incidents relating to the Little People, to Flessie, and to Bigfoot. And we're just getting warmed up.

So we'll add one more, a mystery that involves a sheep dog named Shep, who spent the final years of his life in Fort Benton where so much of Montana's history took place.

The mystery dates to 1936, when Shep arrived in town in the company of his master, a sheepherder who fell ill while tending his flock. The sick sheepherder was lodged at St. Clare Hospital, but no thought was given to his companion, a furry black-and-white canine. While awaiting the release of his master, Shep loitered for days, waiting patiently at the hospital door. One kind nun who ran the kitchen occasionally fed him a plate of leftovers.

Following the death of the sheepherder, family members apparently requested that his body be shipped east by railcar. On an August day, Shep watched as an undertaker rolled a gurney bearing a casket across the station platform where it was loaded aboard the luggage car. Attendants at the station recall that Shep was so distressed that he began whining when the door was slammed shut and the train slowly departed the station. They also describe the distraught pup trotting briefly down the tracks after the train. Certain that his master would return, Shep went back to the station and began a five-and-a-half-year vigil.

He became a fixture on the platform, and the unofficial greeter of the four trains that arrived at the station every day. He stood watching as passengers dismounted, hoping for the arrival of his master. At first he was chased away by the railroad employees; but he eventually became their ward, and they provided him with food and shelter.

As word of his vigil spread across the land, Shep attained celebrity status. In 1938 he was featured in *Ripley's Believe It or Not,* and rail travelers reportedly took long detours off the main line to stop in Fort Benton. Shep began receiving fan mail from school children and gifts at Christmas.

Sadly, the aging process and cold winters took their toll on the pup. He became stiff legged and hard of hearing and, on January 12, 1942, failed to hear the roar of engine number 235 as it rolled into the station at 10:17 A.M. The engine was almost upon Shep—and he was moving out of its way—when he slipped on the icy rails, and his long watch ended. His death also altered the life of the train's engineer, who refused to drive the Fort Benton route again.

The following day, news of Shep's death and an obituary were carried on the wires of the Associated Press and United Press International. With hundreds of mourners in attendance, a Boy Scout honor guard carried a pine box containing the remains of Fort Benton's famous citizen to a burial plot on a lonely bluff overlooking the train depot. The Great Northern Railroad erected a simple obelisk, with a painted wooden cutout of Shep next to it. Beneath it, white stones spelled out SHEP. Lights illuminated the display at night, and conductors pointed it out to their passengers. Eventually, though, the passenger line stopped coming through Fort Benton, and the grave fell into disrepair.

Then, of course, there's "The Rest of the Story."

Perhaps enlightened by a mention Paul Harvey made of the dog in 1988, a new generation of Shep fans was born. A group of admirers banded together to repair and refurbish Shep's grave, replace the wooden cutout with a painted steel monument, and restore the lights. A small parking area and walking trail were also created. For the fiftieth anniversary of Shep's death, the community of Fort Benton organized a committee to produce a lasting memorial to their famous dog. Using photos of Shep, Montanan Bob Scriver, perhaps the most famous bronze sculptor in the West, created a larger than life-sized statue of the town's famous mutt.

Today, at a peaceful, shady site on the levee in the center of town, Shep's likeness continues its vigil at Shepherd's Court, now the town's focal point. His collar and food dish are nearby on display in the Museum of the Upper Missouri where historian Ken Robison responds to the frequent requests for photos and information. "Within the past year at least a dozen authors have contacted the Overholser Historical Research Center," said Robison. In early 2006, newly elected Governor Brian Schweitzer requested two photos of Shep, which now hang in his office.

In 2005, out of the blue, unsolicited photos of the famous dog began finding their way to Robison. Lindsay Duckett provided a photo of Shep that was taken along the Great Northern tracks. Irene Schanche Boker, whose father Tony Schanche was station agent during the dog's vigil, provided twenty newly dis-

OVERHOLSEN HISTORICAL RESEARCH CENTER

One of Montana's most famous pets, Shep became a well-known and beloved figure at the Fort Benton train platform.

covered photos. And Fred Arnst donated a DVD with 16mm film coverage of Shep taken in 1940.

The mystery? Well, it doesn't amount to much.

Though he is but a minor player in this drama, the identity of Shep's owner is a missing piece in the tale. Historian Robison said he may have been one of two sheepherders who died in the mid-1930s, except their bodies are in a nearby cemetery while Shep's owner's body was shipped back east. Or he may have been one of three cowboys who died and were shipped to points east and south. "I am still trying to determine the sheepherder's identity," Robison said.

You've heard and seen the chronicles of brave and loyal companions like Lassie, Rin Tin Tin, and Old Yeller dramatized in radio and television. But Shep's was a drama played out in real life, the heartbreaking and heartwarming elements accentuated by a little bit of mystery. Like most of Montana's enduring narratives, it's been enough to capture our imaginations all these years later.

BIBLIOGRAPHY

What Happened to Meriwether's Boat?

Camp, Carl, "Journey's End for the Iron Boat," in *We Proceeded On*. Lewis and Clark Trail Heritage Foundation, August 2003.

Jackson, Donald. *The Letters of the Lewis and Clark Expedition with Related Documents*. Champaign: University of Illinois Press, 1979.

Moulton, Gary E. *The Definitive Journals of Lewis and Clark*. Lincoln: University of Nebraska Press, 1993.

A Mummy and the Little People

Clark, Ella E. *Indian Legends from the Northern Rockies*. Norman: University of Oklahoma Press, 1966.

Murray, Earl. *Ghosts of the Old West.* New York: Tor Books, 1998.

"The Pedro Mountain Mummy." *The Casper Star-Tribune,* July 22, July 24, 1979.

"The Pedro Mountain Mummy." *The Casper Tribune Herald,* October 22, 1932.

Pittsley, Rich. "Little People: Dressed Like Elvis." *The Billings Outpost,* July 3, 2002.

Smith, Shirley. "The Little People," n.p.

Did Governor Meagher Go Swimming? Or Was He Drowned?

"Accident or Suicide?" *The Eureka Journal,* January 26,1928.

"Account of the Drowning of Gen. Thomas Francis Meagher," in *Contributions to the Historical Society of Montana: Volume 8.* S. Canner and Company, 1966. 131.

Athearn, Robert G. *Thomas Francis Meagher: An Irish Revolutionary in America.* Boulder: University of Colorado Press, 1949.

"The Death of Gen. Thomas Francis Meagher." *Helena Tri-Weekly,* July 6, 1867.

Stevens, Christian D. *Meagher of the Sword*. New York: Mead and Company, 1967.

Was Frank Little Murdered by a Cop?

Axline, Jonathan A. "This is a case for the police." Master's thesis, Montana State University, June 1985.

State of Montana. Certificate of Death, Edward Morrissey. February 6, 1922.

Walter, Dave, ed. *Speaking Ill of the Dead*. Guilford, Conn.: Globe Pequot Press, 2000.

"Who Killed Frank Little?" *Anaconda Standard,* February 2, 1922.

Is the Mystery of the Easton Murder Solved?

"Prolific Robber Found Dead." *The Spokesman-Review,* February 8, 2001.

Was Sheriff Henry Plummer a Highway Robber?

Allen, Frederick. *A Decent, Orderly Hanging*. Norman: University of Oklahoma Press, 2004.

Baumler, Ellen. *Beyond Spirit Tailings.* Helena: Montana Historical Society Press, 2005.

Langford, Nathaniel. *Vigilante Days and Ways.* New York: Grosset and Dunlap, Inc., 1890.

Mather, R. E., and F. E. Boswel. *Hanging the Sheriff.* Salt Lake City: University of Utah Press, 1987.

Is There a Connection Between UFOs and Cattle Mutilations?

"Cattle mutilations back: Ranchers, lawmen baffled by crime wave." *Great Falls Tribune,* January 3, 2002.

Donovan, Roberta, and Keith Wolverton. *Mystery Stalks the Prairies.* Raynesford, Mont.: T.H.A.R. Institute, 1976.

National Institute for Discovery Science. "Summary Report on a Wave of UFO/Helicopters and Animal Mutilations in Cascade County, Montana, 1974–1977." Las Vegas, 2002.

If Bigfoot Exists, He Needs a Shower . . .

Big Foot Research Organization database. www.bfro.net.

"Commissioner candidate says he's seen a Bigfoot." *The Hungry Horse News,* May 18, 2006.

Donovan, Roberta, and Keith Wolverton. *Mystery Stalks the Prairies*. Raynesford, Mont.: T.H.A.R. Institute, 1976.

"Is Bigfoot roaming around Kiowa Camp in Blackfeet Country?" *The Glacier Reporter,* March 2, 2006.

"Professor Bigfoot." *Associated Press,* November 4, 2006.

Who Named the Crazy Mountains?

"The Crazy Mountains." Crazy Mountain Museum pamphlet.

Fisher, Vardis. *Mountain Man*. Moscow, Idaho: University of Idaho Press, 1965.

Linderman, Frank Bird, and Plenty-Coups. *Plenty Coups: Chief of the Crows*. Lincoln: University of Nebraska Press, 2002.

"Long on Beauty, Rich in History." *Big Timber Pioneer,* July 9, 1993.

Van Cleve, Spike. *Forty Years' Gatherin's*. Kansas City: Lowell Press, 1977.

Meet Flessie, the Monster of Flathead Lake

Baumler, Ellen. *Beyond Spirit Tailings*. Helena: Montana Historical Society Press, 2002.

Fugleberg, Paul. *Montana Nessie of Flathead Lake.* Polson, Mont.: Treasure State Publishing, 1992.

"Two New Reports of Flathead Monster Surface." *Bigfork Eagle,* August 11, 2005.

"What Are Your Chances of Sighting the Monster?" Laney Hanzel, *Flathead Lake Monitor,* July 1995.

There Are Ghosts in the Butte Archives, Aren't There?

Baumler, Ellen. *Spirit Tailings.* Helena: Montana Historical Society Press, 2005.

Bratlien, Eric. "Investigations: Old Montana Prison," Tortured Souls Investigations Web site: www.tsimt.net.

Erickson, Martin. "Someone To Love Me." Self-published pamphlet.

"Haunted Places in Montana." theshadowlands.net/places/montana.htm.

A Shaggy Dog Story Produces a Mystery

The Story of Shep. Fort Benton: The River Press, n.d.

INDEX

ABOUT THE AUTHOR

Ed Lawrence is a writer and photographer based in Bozeman, Montana. He combines his passion for flyfishing with work for major magazines. He is also the author of *Frommer's Guide to Montana and Wyoming* and *Frommer's Guide to Yellowstone and Grand Teton National Parks.*